Marianne Faithfull's Cigarette

Marianne Faithfull's Cigarette

Gerry Gomez Pearlberg

CLEIS

Published in the United States by Cleis Press Inc., P.O. Box 14684, San Francisco, CA 94114.

Printed in the United States.

Cover design: Scott Idleman
Text design: Karen Huff
Cleis Press logo art: Juana Alicia

First Edition.

10 9 8 7 6 5 4 3 2 1

Library of Congress Cataloging-in-Publication Data

Pearlberg, Gerry.
  Marianne Faithfull's Cigarette / by Gerry Gomez Pearlberg. — 1st ed.
     p.   cm.
  ISBN 1-57344-034-5 (trade paper)
  I. Title.
PS3566.E2183M37   1998
811'.54 — dc21   97-47575
                                                            CIP

Some of these poems were first published in the following magazines and anthologies: *Chelsea, The Beloit Poetry Journal, The James White Review, Art & Understanding, Apalachee Quarterly, Plazm, The Café Review, Pucker Up, Global City Review, The Lesbian Review of Books, Women's Writes, Calyx, Excursus, Long Shot, modern words, Between the Cracks, The Arc of Love, Tangled Sheets, My Lover Is a Woman, Butch/Femme: Theorizing Lesbian Gender,* and *Portraits of Love.* Many thanks to the editors of these collections for their support.

CONTENTS

III. Cumulonimbus

IV. The Light Moving Behind It

Acknowledgments

My gratitude goes to my friends and fellow poets who critiqued the manuscript, offered encouragement, and kept me afloat: Nayland Blake, Mary Beth Caschetta, Justin Chin, Karen Cook, Stephanie Gilman, Walter Holland, Michelle Karlsberg, Joan Larkin, Andrea Lockett, Elizabeth Pincus, Elizabeth Randolph, Linda Smukler, Kitty Stewart, Cheryl Boyce Taylor, Eva Yaa Asantewaa, and Stephen Wilder. Many others, not named here, have also blessed me with their friendship: you know who you are, and I thank you.

Linda L. Nelson and Tristan Taormino deserve special thanks for their divine interventions. I am also grateful to Cleis Press for taking the plunge on this books of poems.

I want also to acknowledge the impact of my too-brief friendship with M. Brooks Jones (1944-1989). His creative passion, even in the face of debilitating illness, has been a lasting example that's kept me writing.

Three teachers—Alan Zeigler (then of Teachers & Writers Collaborative), Frank McCourt, and Christine Stansell—at very different points, in times long past, offered mentorship and friendship on which I continue to draw to this day.

And I bow in respect to Otto, my muse.

I

MARIANNE FAITHFULL'S CIGARETTE

MARIANNE FAITHFULL'S CIGARETTE

It was on the floor, being X-ed out by her long
black heel, infinite and doomed. I had to have it.

Her lips had been around it. Lipstick left on it.
I had to have it. I asked you to get it.

She was raking her fingers through her thin blonde hair.
Glancing up at the ceiling, chain-smoking.

The academics around her were talking, talking, talking.
She gazed up at the ceiling—bored, exhaling.

She rolled her eyes, then looked at us and smirked, you said.
I missed that, pondering the acropolis of fallen cigarettes
        at her feet.

How they looked like smoldering ruins—toppled, scattered.
Broken haloes of a calcified Atlantis.

Pondering chain-smoking. What a beautiful word.
I missed the look she gave us, bemused and bored.

I was thinking about the ring of lipstick on the filter.
I was thinking about the brand, and where she might've
        bought it.

Watching her light up was like seeing the Messiah.
Or Buddha's burning moment under leaves of cool desire.

For L.

THE SEA OF TRANQUILITY

Disappointment is a lesson from Heaven.
—SIGN IN FRONT OF ST. FRANCIS OF ASSISI CHURCH, MANHATTAN

What if you were the lightbulb in a globe,
the light inside a globe of the moon, cervical and contained?
What if you could move toward a point of light without ever
reaching it, perpetual circumnavigation?
You'd be a map of the moon, a mystery of light and place,
mounts and craters named for astronomers and gods.
You'd be a lunar sea waiting for someone to reach you,
to confer upon you a Latinate name,
a desiccated sea languishing for the sensation of tide.

Who identifies and catalogues the lunar scars that decree
the way we live today: for every scar, a name?
Mare Nubium, Sea of Clouds.
Mare Imbrium, Sea of Rains.

Don't you wish you could reach the Sea of Tranquility,
sail through disappointment as if it were mere latitude,
            a finite location with fixed coordinates?

BLUE MOVIE/MOON WALK

Blue Movie/

You turn me on like the star of a blue movie,
five o'clock shadow under a huge blue moon.
Your feminine face all altar boy, eclipse and allure,
your heart a lunar meadow I've no earthly hope of reaching.

We are in your living room watching blue movies.
I adore the term "blue movies," almost as much as I adore
watching you watch them in the dark, voyeur
of your voyeurism: *I love to watch you watch.*

Raven-haired beauties gyrate on the neon screen.
Outside your window blue-black crows begin to speak.

Your black-and-white TV's a small blue moon
perfect for blue movies in the five a.m. dark,
for blue corn chips punctuated by glinting grains of salt,
this moment's room a cool cartoon.

Your baby-powdered body smells like blue.
Our pink cunts swerve like submersibles
 in their deep-sea denim channels
below smooth lagoons of baby blanket blue.

In just two cycles of the moon

we've made love in countless rooms,
pressed against so many walls and floors
like breathless astronauts sealed to one another,
adrift in pale mystery.

/Moon Walk

I will follow you to the end of this film strip
as if it were the landing on the moon:
the reasons for the romance
will, of course, be questioned in the end—
there'll be the usual accusations of falsification
and conspiracy. When it's done
we'll each insist the miracle was staged.

But for now, we're glued to one another's sets,
mesmerized by one another's depths
of touch, each moan an icon,
our lonesome flesh carbonated by static,
eerie lighting and alienated costumes,
an ever-more-abstracted world,
accelerated breath, lack
of oxygen, loss of gravity—
and oh the delirious buoyancy, delicious terror
when the safety-cord frays and there's that sudden flash
of something you have always wanted,
hurtling toward you,
impossibly blue.

THINK BACK

Agnes Moorehead, Hedy Lamarr,
Edith Head, and a smirky beautician
named Madge are in a low-cut car
heading toward the headlands, the outback, the margins.

Heads in the clouds, gloved hands on the wheel,
they're heady with the thrill of an all-girl
American adventure circa 1950-something.
Why not? Life's short.

"Life's short," croons Agnes.
She should know, but that comes later.
Right now everything that matters is in that car.
The breeze is blowing through the front-seat hair
of Edith Head and Hedy Lamarr.
Four single girls on the road for a drive.
Madge's manicured hand riding Agnes' thigh.

Edith leans forward to adjust her tie
and imagines a film that hasn't been
made yet, a movie called *Thelma and Louise*.
Madge and Agnes laugh her off, and Hedy joins in,
roaring as she freshens her face in the rearview mirror.
One eye on the road, she guides the lipstick sprocket
along the pocket of her lips, doesn't miss

a beat driving that stop sign red
around the sarcastic octagon of her mouth,
fully aware of Madge eyeballing her
from the back seat, flooding
with desire, a full tank of gas
sidling up to an easy match.

A girl can't help noticing how
another girl applies her makeup.
Vantage point is everything.

Years from now, Madge will take advantage
of *her* vantage point, sit everyone down around
a crystal ball of blue water, and inform them that
they're "soaking in it."
They'll be appalled, might even shrink back
from imagining too vividly the infamous
Moorehead deathbed scene—two rival lovers (both
bombshell legends) in the hospital room
mopping her brow, pondering the will,
recalling the taut infusions of lipstick,
mascara, and eau de cologne on the sheets
and pillowcases of other, non-deathbed beds.
Yes, they, like everyone else, are "soaking in it."

But all that comes later.
Right now is its own cliff-hanging time and place,

its own quickly driven moment,
with a Continuity Lady called Today
and a Script Girl named Mañana.

DIETRICH'S SWAN SONG

They applauded their hearts out at her final performance
She wore a full-length swan down cape
because someone once promised that swan down
    would sparkle
like the stars in a snow bank on the darkest of nights

Dietrich wore a full-length swan down cape
swigged a bottle of Dom before the rise of the curtain
like a star in a snow bank on the darkest of nights
alone in the dressing room before her last show

Swigged Dom Pérignon before the rise of the curtain
and sent smoke rings like sea wreaths twisting in air
alone in the dressing room before the last show
seeing the smoke in the mirror was like seeing underwater

Smoke rings like sea wreaths twisting in air
or swans craning their necks toward some strange apparition
seeing the smoke in the mirror was like seeing underwater
there were visions to be given by the genie in her bottle

Swans craning their necks toward a strange apparition
who ardently swore that her swan down would sparkle
like reversed mirror visions of genies in bottles
clapping their hearts out at her final performance.

THE DEATH OF SUPERMAN

Remember that first tumble?
The one you took through space in a basket
like Moses through the dark wet channel of the midnight sky?
How those *My Favorite Martian* radio signals
clung to their oxygen tanks like
stars turning dime-store gold
on the undrinkable reservoirs of this daily planet?
Tonight, the American flag
over the Exxon station is so huge
that it frightens you as you pull off
the highway of angels.
You've reached the other side
of all your tumbling battles, Superman:
this town is Retrospect, a place to hang your hat.

And when the test comes back from the neon lab,
and when the waiting room waits for something good
        to happen,
and when the arms of Lois Lane
pan your sky like lighthouse beacons in the night,
and when she kisses you and calls you "Clark"—
how vividly you can imagine what it is to lose everything,
how graphic, how lustrous, how radiant the fear.

Loss is a one-night stand on an empty runway,

a white calla lily simmering in your hand.
Wave it in the air: surrendering flag.
Dangle it to the ground: trumpet for the lips of your heart.

Signatures of blood claim credit for catastrophe,
run rivulets down your face like an eyeliner masque.
As your body has completed the work of your mind,
your mind has exerted itself against your flesh.
The calla lily seems to mourn you,
its buried trumpet calcifying
in the underground cake of minerals and stethoscopes,
its tongue the color of dried ice,
a passenger pigeon pressed like a primrose
between the pages of a hardbound book.

You're that calla lily, Clark,
a series of dots torn from the page,
reconnecting in the night sky,
a blind constellation of heroic service
popped from your frame.
Take off your glasses,
your wristwatch, your tie.
You won't be needing them, man of steel.
Take off your shoes, those pants,
the red and blue spandex, the yellow belt,
the tattooed *S* on the tattoo of you.
Take back your body.

Touch it with your hands as if for the first time.
This is the first time.
Watch yourself in the mirror.
Turn off those X-ray eyes and what do you see?

You are naked
and your hair is
a blue-black crow
in a cypress
preening in the dark.

Remember its color.
Everything must die.

JECKYLL GARDEN

Hard to keep one's mind
off his body's dying. How kind
he was to animals, how good
with flowers. Him in a chair
in his best friend's garden.
The Victorian shimmer of ostracized
roses, late single-bloomers.
Hectic spread of king-fisted sunflowers
nodding out in a fever
of seedy orange glare
that even blue hydrangea's
gluey islands could not cool.
Sunlight particles
riveted to one side
of a tall blue spruce
like barnacles.
And walls of morning
glory like rows
of frosted shotglasses
on the shelves of his saloon:
his glass of lemonade, glistening.

Beyond the din of bumblebees, ocean din.
Sounds peeling back from other sounds like insect skins.

THE SHE-MARINER

[Coney Island, 1932]

She sails over gender,
and it over her—
a candied apple glaze,
stiff men's suit.

Fried clams
are her currency,
a soft molten coinage
in which ancient Roman profiles
rise up in battered beer.

She's got the ocean
in her pocket, neatly
folded, men's handkerchief
or map.

Almost nothing
is a mystery to her now—

except perhaps
the dozen roses, pupa-white,
clenched in the florist window

at the corner of Mermaid & Neptune.

LOOP-THE-LOOP IN PROSPECT PARK (1905)

I.

The early evening hill is a lantern's lamp
nightly relumed with a golden match.

From here I watch the families traverse
the Long Meadow paths like ants

with empty picnic baskets and wide black prams,
scurrying home before the oncoming dark.

They barely notice me reclined upon this hill
observing their departures amidst a spreading quietude,

at once random and precise: it stills the park
benches, the lily pond, the lindens and the elms—

and the row boats hitched to the silver firs
that batten down Swan Boat Lake's shore,

hull clanking hull as if to entice the by-the-hour
and half-day renters—even the Lullwater

Creek that feeds the lake subdues
its anxious murmurings

in deference to the tranquilizing night.
In the evening some things vanish

and other things grow clear. Succulent aromas
impinge on air: night-blooming trees

repeal the scent of frankfurters and beer.
That's when we appear,

emerging from what conceals
and thus releases us: wood glens

dark as apothecary phials, dense hydrangea
fortresses that wreathe the fields

in folded maps of powder blue—the fountains
in the Vale Cashmere, the Vale's blurred

hedge of rose and bittersweet and rose,
the glade of bamboo slivers that skirts the Nethermead,

and the cattails that eclipse the marsh's bank,
obscuring the limits of its amphibious border,

its miracles of ambidextrous reach.
At these apertures of dusk, we wait.

II.

I've paid those cops quite handsomely
to let me be while wearing this dress,

this purse, these fine white women's gloves.
I've paid them handsomely

to be a fairy in Prospect Park at dusk
in my dress, hat, stockings, gloves.

The boys call me "Loop-the-loop" like the Coney Island ride—
ten times the thrill at a somewhat higher price.

III.

Our joke is that they call it "Prospect Park" because it's here
the trade is best: older gentlemen stroll the open fields

with Bungalow Bar or pipe in hand, lingering
by benches: patient, well-mannered, self-possessed,

eager to purchase what the poor-but-pretty will purvey—
though too many come with illusions of finding love for free.

Me? I've got love at home—a charm-school faun,
dreamy boy whom I adore.

This is business, like those swan boats for hire
waiting in the shallows for the chance

to guide or be guided into deeper waters.
But beyond the money that's in it,

there's pleasure too, when a moan
is delivered into the dark

or a sigh to the ear like an envelope.
Inside the tunnel of the Endale Arch

stir nightly echoes of delirium's touch
that even terror of disgrace cannot disarm.

IV.
I remember one warm October night
meeting an uncommonly handsome man

by the swell of purple ironweed near Music Island
where the wealthy take in after-supper shows:

the sky seemed extra-wide—a vagrant shield of sky—
into which darkness exhaled all its glistening stars:

it was one good night: soft sentiment
alighting like dragonflies

before money passed from hand to hand.
Long after money, there's memory's romance:

it pleases me to think of all the men who'll think of me
on lonely nights beneath the spread of other, less
    compelling skies.

V.

Morning dew, I've learned here, isn't *morning* dew at all—
it falls at night, while meteors fall.

I can't begin to count the stars that I've watched glide
across Brooklyn's endless sky—nor the nights

I've lain in the arms of men—some lovely, some tender,
some grudging—on grassy beds incandesced

by dew as night's cool astronomy lays low
and the horse-drawn carriages begin their ride

through the park's dim carriage roads, and the
trolley cars plunge the hill to Flatbush

Avenue on steel scars re-incised
by morning's light. By that awakening world

beyond the margins of this park,
we mark our time. Soaked like nymphs

and Neptunes, we compose ourselves and rise
from the foamy smell of semen

like the Coney Island tide, when the sun tosses out
her first white net, and the schools of fish,

still sleeping, are confounded by the light.
It's then, before returning home

to the faun's warm, rumpled bed
that I stroll back to this hill to watch

my loose, unchartered club of men
drift like inky phantoms from the park—

past the Comfort Stations where the east and west
drives meet, beyond the Doric Shaft,

Monument to Sailors and Soldiers,
dispersing at last at Grand Army Plaza,

baptized by the shadow of its high, Triumphal Arch.

II

HEAVEN Y HIELO

SAILOR

The girls go by in their sailor suits
They catch my eye in their sailor suits
Big or slight they all grin like brutes
In steam-ironed pants and buffed jet boots
They saunter right up my alley.

I study their easy, confident strides
Crew cuts and white hats capping decadent eyes
They shiver the pearl on night's oystery prize
They shiver me timbers, unbuckle me thighs
This alley was made for seething.

From the sweat of a street lamp or lap of the sea
A smooth sailor girl comes swimming to me
Says she wants it right now and she wants it for free
Clamps her palms to my shoulders, locks her knees
        to my knees
This alley was made for cruising.

Her face is dark coffee, her head has no hair
Her cap shines like neon in the bristling night air
She pins her brass metals to my black brassiere
Tucks her teeth like bright trophies behind my left ear
This alley is very rewarding.

She tosses her jacket and rolls up her sleeve
On her arm's a tattoo of an anchor at sea
She points to the anchor and whispers, "That's me."
And the wetter I get the more clearly I see
This alley was made for submersion.

Her fingers unbutton my 501's
This girl's fishing for trouble and for troubling fun
She slides off her gold rings and they glint like the sun
Then she smirks, rubs her knuckles, and spits out her gum
This alley was made for swooning.

Now she's pushing her prow on my ocean's sponge wall
Uncorking my barnacle, breaking my fall
And there's pink champagne fizzling down my decks
    and my hall
As she wrecks her great ship on my bright port-of-call
This alley was made for drowning.

DOG STAR

How that girl can move
on this white-hot
San Francisco day's high noon
I'll never know.
Treeless, blunt savannah air
bends like clumps of batter
in my wire-whisking stare.
Today it's like a desert here.

Her millet-colored van's a secret cave.
She always enters from the rear.
Her slow crawl toward the dashboard
is a choppy filmstrip, sand and white,
scratched up by the trickle of her clean blade knife
and glare that alternately shows and fades
the paper bag of bones between her teeth,
her hind legs flexing in the spotted shade.

She's a brass hyena uncaking a cool dirt den,
a wild mutt muscling her way from a wire pen.

The sun throws constellations
on the hood and rearview mirror of her van.
She curls against the window pane—
bleached hair, tan shirt and

sandy cheeks like native relics under glass,
and finally in the mashing heat she sleeps,
a tough glazed donut in the driver's seat.

Tethered by bright chains of canine dreams,
she twitches, growls, and snaps at each.

I watch her, straining at my leash.

THE BOXERS AND THE FISHERDYKE

The Boxerdyke
walks her boxer dog
wearing polka dotted
boxer shorts.

The dog wears a collar
with metal spikes.
The same is said
of the Boxerdyke.

Both have close-cropped ears
and crew cut hair
and prideful,
penetrating stares.

They both eat meat,
they're both called "Butch,"
so it's sometimes hard
to tell which is which.

The Boxerdyke
takes her boxer pal
when she cruises the alley
for available gals.

It's often been told
that their alley cat ways
have caused dyke and dog both
to end up far astray.

For the alley's not far
from the Fisherdyke's wharf
and Fisherdyke is well known
for reeling boxers off course.

She's been watching these boxers
for a very long while
she likes boxer dog's looks
and Boxerdyke's feral style.

So she's devised a temptation,
an allure lure, fail-safe
made of treasure-hunt gems
leading right to her place.

She has littered the alley
with irresistible things:
red wax lips, lacy slips,
mood and decoder rings.

There are water guns, dice,
corn cob pipes, cowboy hats,

silver rocket-shaped dildoes,
pink champagne, whiffle bats.

Fisherdyke bides her time
by her boxes of hooks,
reels, lines, sinkers and rods.
She sits reading pulp books

Till the Boxerdyke bites
till she nibbles the bait;
Fisherdykes are quite patient,
boxers being worth the wait.

So when Boxerdyke next
in her striped boxer shorts
takes her boxer dog Butch
for their evening cavort

She's soon hot on the trail
of a grand shopping spree
that begins with some glossies
of Miss Peggy Lee.

She finds hand-beaded leashes,
Jughead caps, Archie comics,
Lincoln Logs, Tarot cards,
leather bras and hair tonics.

There are black latex gloves
that pull up the shoulders,
leopard print dental dams,
pearl-white cigarette holders.

Soon she's nearing her destiny
her arms full of prizes—
even Butch lends a hand
with his jowly incisors.

Boxerdyke barely notices
when she reaches the dock,
she's absorbed with the trail
of Tinker Toys and pink clocks.

Boxerdyke nears the shack,
boxer dog close behind,
they lay down their huge cache
hoping more waits inside—

And they're right in that way
only boxers can be
swinging open the door
they're delighted to see

Fisherdyke with long dreadlocks
tying violet trout flies

looking up from her work
with a bright, sexy smile.

Fisherdyke wears a wetsuit
since she dives all the time
she's a pearl-diving girl
and her aim's so sublime

that Boxerdyke is soon pinned
to the sea captain's bed
Fisherdyke keeps her there
with moist lips and salt dreads.

Fisherdyke holds her close
till Boxerdyke feels the prod
of Fisherdyke's sexy lines,
and well-endowed fishing rod.

But Boxerdyke's most enthralled
by Fisherdyke's clever sport
when Fisherdyke slips her hands
down Boxerdyke's boxer shorts.

SHAVE

The flea market razor
will do. We'll do it
with the silver
heavy-handled one:
a force of nature,
organic in my hand.
In an old wooden bowl
warm water,
shaving brush,
and soap will
whip a froth amalgam
blinding white
as winter in
a wintermint canoe.

Tip up your handsome chin.

I'll slush
a slash of foam
across your cheek,
but just for fun:
tonight, my girl,
we'll row out
past the crew cut
docked upon your shore

and pull this silver
oar across your heady
waves of auburn grain
to leave a smooth
stone polished in its wake,
organic in its purity of form.

FIRST DATE WITH THE D.J.

We were in Brooklyn.
Her hand was on my thigh
when we pulled up to the stop sign.
The boys on the corner shouted
"Bulldykes!" and in a flash
she pulled a gun
from her glove compartment
and waved it like a hand-puppet
till they were history.
"They need to know we're armed and dangerous," she said.

We pulled up to my house.
There was a ruby slipper between my thighs,
a poppy field in the back of my brain
though Kansas might as well have been a globe away.
By the time she pulled my sweater off
under the street lamp
and kissed me in that glow,
I could barely remember
the name those kids had called us,
what a gun was, or how to speak
the language we'd been speaking
all our lives.

AFTER JAMES LAUGHLIN'S
"IN ANOTHER COUNTRY"

Her eyes were the color
of a Timberland boot:
suede-gold, gecko-cool.
Too tired to smile but not to
stare, we grazed each other
as if eye contact were a
contact sport, something
you needed a license for—
say, bass fishing the glades
of public lands. The train
squirmed into its tunnel
like an endangered eel,
dimmed, and slunk
back out again.
Everything seemed then
to expand: daylight streamed
into the car and with it
sky, skyline, a bewildering
plate-glass metropolis.
Her glance a goblet:
over-full, spillable,
the city itself.
Our orange plastic
seats seemed suddenly

modern, spanking clean,
and we at last
alert, alive—
viable!—
our windows pried open.
Tight as a barnacle against
my drift, she was, so that people
stared, and suddenly seemed
much older than my 19 years,
halfway to thirty-eight, an age
as abstract then
as solitary confinement.
Back in the tunnel,
the lights bobbed on and
off, mournful ships at
mourning sea. Her thigh
pressed mine, corduroy
collage—ropey water, a warm, sudsy chafe.
The train lurched to a
stop between untiled stations.
Lights browned down to sepia
shade, and the engine went
dead while ceiling fans
ineffectually whirred as if
trying to keep themselves
awake. One could almost
count backwards to the days

of nickel fares and wicker seats.
Her body an unseen
cicada, mumbling: invention
of soundwave, branch, and air. I
no longer cared who saw what or
what they saw. At 19,
what I'd never even thought
to dream was finally
happening to me.
I imagined apple orchards,
a buck bumping antlers
against a lichen-brittle branch:
divining rods seeking divining
rods amidst shiny balloons
of fruit in a too-cool
fall. Restored to life,
the train again propelled us
through Brooklyn or the notion
of it, and by the time it came
time for her stop, her stop
was also mine. I
strolled off behind
her, the way I'd heard
of men tumbling
after men in the park,
followed her up
escalators of tarnished

steel and thumbprint rubber,
into a neighborhood that
smelled like the river
and sloped that way along
side streets fixed in time.
At the piers, painstaking waves
slapped and slapped the docks
whose wooden cylinders were plush
with immersion, wreathed
in velveteen algae to which
clung starfish the color of exit
signs. Together we stared into
the perseverant river, into
the faces of everyone
we'd ever loved, in
English or Italian,
then lost again.
The dead were especially vivid,
their faces insulated by sketchy
thumbnail waves, bronze and
shimmering, amaretto-scented.
She said, *The river responds*
to nothing and to everything;
I wonder if that frustrates them.
But their faces were bright and mask-like,
well beyond worry, as if encased in a sugar glaze
which the waves appeared to linger over,

smoothing their cracks and wrinkles caressingly
until the faces were entirely gone
and she and I returned
from our abandonment of reveries
to one another. She tossed
her thick brown wallet
onto the pier.
It flapped like a fish.
Still clothed, she dove
into the river, wet cotton
warping on her skin
like a walrus' loose-fitting fur.
Down in the water, her face seemed doubly wide: Volatile.
Mammalian.
The color teal impaled her.
Light's tiny tines pricked
the waves about
her shoulders like Neptune's
spears. I wonder
if they hurt her, or if the sea
gulls did, appearing out of
nowhere and diving
at her as if
she were an unexpected spill
of baby shrimp, pinkly
translucent, first learning
to squirm in a sudden thaw.

She curved
and uncurled like a
shrimp with horsewhip
antennae, bulleting
downward and deep away
toward the tentacle libraries of the sea.

I regretted not having a tail or a ticket
to take the ride she offered
to a place where I envisioned
the violent suction
of masks removed and Real
Faces—familiar—finally
reconciled
to an endlessly
collapsible, impending past.

FOR BRANDON TEENA

Were you buried in your favorite slacks,
black cowboy shirt, and cowboy hat?
That's what the papers said (at first).
Or were you laid to rest in a women's
flowered print, a "ladies'" blouse,
as your relatives insisted that
the *Lincoln Journal* print
in their "correction" of the "facts"
of how you dressed—alive *and* dead?

Are any of us what our families pretend?
Our sex lives and the nature of our deaths
reclaimed, revisited, unread—
unspeakable what we do in bed
and whom we love and how we dress,
encountering eternity in our favorite slacks,
cowboy shirts and vests and hats.
Confronting eternity undisguised.
Dressed to kill. To die for. *Unrevised.*

POISON ARROW TREE FROGS

Roots rise
like dark umbrella muscles
from the soil.
Flowers bloom in air.
Ruby tree frogs haul
their eggs upon their backs,
raise young in puddled pools
inside the flutes
of champagne-vialed blooms
a half a mile above the forest floor.
And carry poison in their skin.

Next time it rains at night,
I'll pack a picnic snack
of Cupid's darts
and lure you to the park,
embrace you hard
against a wet and shining branch
and let the texture
of the dark, the rain,
the bark absorb us,
poised and panting,
naked, stark.

I knew a girl whose fingers widened at the tips,

like suction pads.
In her lush room I climbed the ceiling
while those fingers climbed my wall
and wet eurythmic music sprayed
a repetitious, aching phrase like
all the sex I'd ever have
and ever want
and ever go to jail
and lose my friends
and civil rights
and safety for.

Entire species of experience
pass into extinction,
unnoticed:
Her touch evaporating from my skin.
My touch dampening yours.
And all those other signs of life and breath and flesh
the world'll never care to know.

HAPPY BIRTHDAY, BABY

Was I handcuffed, John?

No, baby,
you were wearing restraints,
the leather ones, and you
were on your belly,
with the full head-hood.

John wrote *It's my birthday: Fuck me.*
across my back in purple wax
and sent a stranger in to do the job.

Remember when we saw our bodies
as perfect, untouchable things,
seashells on shelves,
silvery souvenirs
that nothing could mar?

THE CIRCLE BEING DESCRIBED

It's old but reliable
so when summer comes
it's on my window sill,
wide black blades churning
the luminous night like catfish circling in a silver bucket,
skin-soaked angels describing heaven's small circumference.

There's something beyond heroic
about lasting all this time: this was
my grandmother's fan, a 1940s purchase made
on Steinway Street in the heat of Astoria's August
following a night so humid it's famous in our family—
Grammy kept awake by the frantic knocking of
back-alley June bugs flicking themselves
like burnt brown matches against the window screens.

They ached for artificial light,
she said, just as she longed
for a sleep-inducing breeze.

I know that aching too,
not for sleep, but for
a certain kind of light.
I strain against the sense
that survival from that time to this

is something sacred, strain
for the lost faith in a future tense
that, citizen of the plague, I can barely conceive.

The ghosts of my grandmother's day
and now, too many ghosts of mine,
reside in boiling whirlpools
of angry air and light.
I feel them when I lie awake
in this heated breeze that does not dream.
I feel them breathe on me, the exhale of their wings.

Their aching pressed on aching pressed against my
        metal screen.

JACK DEMPSEY

a boxer
but also
a fish:
silver-cheeked
mash-jawed
eyes like specks of gravel
on a fish tank floor.

the mat is red
the gloves are plum
the rope is white
the crowd is pump-like:
water churning through charcoal,
a roiling boil.

if you were
a fish what
would you hear
or want to listen to?
plate glass
a kind of inner
ear, filtering
this world from
the next one.

a knock-out
punch bruises.
a blood clot bell
yawns whirlpooled
mucous on a mat
of scarlet gill.

it's midnight
in the holding tank
& Jack Dempsey,
down & out
& oxygen prone,
longs to
hurl himself
over the
plate glass rim,
to aim a dorsal fin
at that next
great
maybe world,
leaving behind
a starry trail
of blood,
multicolored
gravel,
& fame

on the lemon shag carpet
in the living room ring.

OLD YELLER WALL PAPER

Like that good old dog
they had to shoot
there are different ways
of carving up
the heart's dead weight:
chronology, trauma, deceit,
and burnt-umber grief
linger like lockets
you lost the key to,
still chained
around your neck.

Sometimes, no matter
how wrong it might be,
it just feels
too good to stop.
Today's the kind of day
you'd take a dog out
to be shot,
foaming at the mouth.

Fear's like wall paper,
hue upon peeling hue:
velvet ivy borders,
floral stains,

nose-diving dogs.
Underneath the underneath
inky glue is smeared
along four walls
that cradle and confine.
The soul's thin halls
are membrane keyholes
you can listen
through. Many
layers, many hues.

Steam the heart open
like an envelope.
It's all floral disasters, ivy
chokers and
dirt hounds
salivating for some
abstract bone
a million miles
from home.

Layers of paper
line the walls of rooms
you used to live through.

Wishful thinking
is a room that does

not fit inside itself,
floors akimbo, windows overblown.
Desire is the doghouse of the heart
gnawing on its paw.

It's no different
across town:
there the heart is also,
and also there.
Across the blue ocean,
it crosses the street
without holding your hand.
It foams at the mouth,
and is nothing more
than motor pulse,
voluntary and
involuntary spasms
set off by bright electrolytes: yeah,
sometimes
the hard facts
soothe us,
other times they're
like a yellow dog
dragged by its collar
out back
behind the shed,

called out back
by love, rubbed
on the ear
by the ambidextrous
thumb of love

then shot,
real quick,
dead on.

THE NATIONAL COUNCIL OF JEWISH WOMEN'S THRIFT SHOP

on Flatbush Avenue
is run by a bunch
of tough old gals
who chain-smoke
(unfiltered) brands
you never even
heard of
leaning on the
counter display
of ladies'
handkerchiefs and
costume jewelry
(undersea-world-
of-Jacques-Cousteau
greens and blues,
pigments of hard
candy, mouthwash,
Beeman's gum).

Blue smoke swims
through strands of
bluish hair.
An instant coffee
jar stuffed full

of pearl-blue hatpins:
clusters of pale
roe in moving water.
A dyke in a fez
inspects flannel
men's pajamas,
fingering mustard polka
dots, whirling amoebic
swirls, hardening
elastic waistbands.
A mustached muscle
man cruises the racks
for something to go
with that trashy
lemon-yellow evening
gown still muffy
with mothballs.

No one's watching,
mister, so go ahead
and bury your
face in that
polymorphous chiffon,
sink to your knees and breathe
that long, solitary breath
of crinoline and lace
that's like drowning

in the most marvelously
queeny ocean
tuned to the exact
temperature of your body
where time's suspended
and beauty holds its breath
where style and language
money and despair
are somebody else's problem,
and—for the moment, anyway—
no one's putting you through hell.

THE MARRIAGE OF HEAVEN Y HIELO:
A LOVE NARRATIVE OF SORTS

Think well and be a king,
Think more and think again

—GERTRUDE STEIN, FROM "BEFORE THE FLOWERS OF FRIENDSHIP FADED
FRIENDSHIP FADED"

Benson & Hedges swap candycorn hats,
leopard-spotted leotards,
leather caps, Orangina
tutus, and semiotic big black boots.

Benson & Hedges: two marshmallows on a stick
impaled by fire.

Benson says: *Long live the King.*
King = top of the lesbian crop.

Benson's got a thing for King.
Hedges goes along for the ride.

King is an apothecary of desire, flooded
with rose-tinted cross-bone syrups
that magically transgress
to coughdrop green in bottles
hung from cage-like ceiling slings

of silver chain. King
paces her telescopic castle halls
of fanfare and fan tracery,
hourglasses, measuring cups,
and flasks of sleeping tongue.

Benson & Hedges, whose brains are blades,
glide toward the castle gate
wearing armors of intent for their
double date with destiny.
Their lives a skating rink,
their silver blades saw stories into ice
flicking grit and ice cubes
in each other's eyes: those cocktail
party sound effects of desire pouring in.

King is a cold fish, an effigy of herself on fire.
Burning always (or so it seems) on someone else's castle wall.

Desire is more than lipstick and a mouth.
It gnaws at Benson from the inside out.
False teeth, saber-tooth Swiss Army knives,
bicuspids, cupid's bows.
Benson has no date of birth, no ID card.
No beginning, middle, or end to what she wants,
that spiraling infinity of the reaching
for the out-of-reach.

King, an icon herself,
has a shelf of unwanted icons:
pin-headed dolls from ex's who hate her,
holograms from the scenes of the crime,
and a tarnished crown that whispers "Don't ask."

Sometimes King would like to rearrange her furniture:
replace the love seat with a single bed, toss out
the horsewhip and the other princely props,
pinprick the royal velvet cushions, deflate
the pedestal and throne. It's lonely being a top.

Sometimes Benson wishes an older, wiser Benson
would take matters into her own hands,
but that would be like putting a gun
to her head, blowing away the stellar
system of everything she knows
she cannot have, that parallel universe
of not-so-laughable lapses that always
seem to keep her
in the game.

Desire waves from the castle gate like a monogrammed hanky.
The initials keep changing but the script's always the same:
handwriting of a lonely girl trying to live up to being King.
It isn't easy being a man. It isn't easy being on top.

Tonight, the stars hovering by King's castle are alchemical,
an unfamiliar alphabet
                    souping down a river
                                    of new water,
                                            a new water
one can skate across,
soft water transmuting all-too-readily to gold.
The night is a moat with a drawbridge that says:
        Identify yourself to the dark.

King is a constellation shifting in the sky.
On this and every other night she'll sleep
and rise
with both boots on.
It isn't easy being the cream of the crop
and it's lonely, lonely, lonely
at the top.

III

CUMULO-
NIMBUS

THRUSH

The Central Park Rambles
rush with bird songs
trickling through pines,
a kind of uncovering, a lifting off of stones.

Last year Jay was harassed here,
for cruising, by an officer of the law:
"What's the matter, pretty boy—AIDS got your tongue?"

Jay held his ground in silence,
projecting himself into the unexpected music
of a distant hermit thrush,
a rare bird rarely heard to sing.

This year, Jay is in St. Luke's
with a case of thrush that makes it
hard for him to speak.
The yellow fungus on his lips
makes him look like a fledgling,
open-mouthed, awaiting the arrival
of a saving grace poised in the air
between talons of light.

Propped up in bed, between sips of soda
from a straw, he rambles about "apocalypse ecology,"

gesturing at the evidence, a nest
of *Newsday* clippings: dogs
leaping from high rises, disappearing frogs,
and the drastic decline of song birds in America.

Throat swelled with sphagnum,
legs cracked to the texture of red birch,
head increasingly in the clouds—
so he is becoming the tree of his own falling life,
a favorite of the minor gods:
north side moss,
south side hardened bark,
sensation unpeeling from his limbs like leaves.

STILL LIFE OF OTTO

[In the voice of an older man. After Jan Morris's Conundrum*]*

How young, how pale.
He stood in the plate glass doorway
half evolved in harbor shadows,
his broken hair, tangled belly
and roast duck shoes
thrust out, almost flying,
lopsided game birds flung from Maltese hooks.
Egypt, May 6, 1945.

Cherishing my pining
after all these dark marsh years,
I relish still the thump of homosexual instinct,
the secret grotto of his caress,
quizzical, suppressed,
his chalk's insistent rubbing
at my table's white silk slate.

The overturning of an oil lamp
sent a dark Aladdin stain
across the front of his soft pants.

And the stubble stippling blue
the puzzle of his cheeks and chin

held precious as the book of psalms
between my adolescent palms.
The harbor mist was like a sponge
we swabbed between our naked chests
his breasts were rosy candle flames
snuffed out by my young tongue
the night before
my nineteenth birthday,
May of 1945.

CUMULONIMBUS

[The red plastic apostrophe has fallen from the Sloane's Supermarket sign on Fourteenth Street and Seventh Avenue in Manhattan's West Village. It lies on the ground like a giant comma between this world and another.]

The day drones on.

Leaning against the wall
cigarette perched on lips,
Cumulonimbus at the snow-bound grave
of fallen Apostrophe
ponders the limits of possessiveness,
Freud's narcissism of white sleep.

A cloud hauled down by brute force to an earthbound temple
is trampled by silver foxes, stallions of ice.

Cumulonimbus says: *There's the night we die*
                       and the night behind our death.
                       It's that second night
                       that calls us like a master
                       from our lives.

Cumulonimbus runs
out of cigarettes

at the snow-bound grave.
Birds fly from pockets
into smoke nests dangling in air.

Handsome Stanza strolls by
with a giant poodle
the color of the Parachute
Jump at Sodom-by-the-Sea.
Ignorant of irony, resentment,
and the other romance languages,
young Stanza turns Cumulo's head.

A wistful Cumulonimbus murmurs:

> *Sometimes we miss our viscous poisons,*
> *in their vials so divine!*

[In memory of Michael Callen]

LOST IN SPACE

What else was there for Doctor Smith to do but lead
       that poor Will Robinson astray?
It was in the script as much as in the stars,
the casting couch as constellation, a formidable religion.

If every family needs a foil, who better than effeminate
Doctor Smith, who snuck aboard their space craft uninvited,
an alien interloping on an alien world.

Everyone knows that only certain households have a
       claim to heaven.
Even Doctor Smith—*especially* Doctor Smith—knows that.
So it's no surprise that only the gullible early-model robot
of limited I.Q. and that precocious kid will have anything
to do with him. It's his fault they're lost.
And his fault they're never found.

Which is why he huddles alone in his narrow cabin
on a tiny cot with silvery thermal sheets drawn up
to the chin, holding forth against the strange and mysterious
elements of these repositioned nights
in space, eyes terrified and wide.
The constellations are lean-tos in a black forest,
propping up a whole other universe, a whole other night sky.
It's those other worlds that worry him: worlds,

like Earth, that can never be home to him again.
There, as here, he's always someone else's metaphor
for limp-wristed cowardice, intrusion, vice.
A foreign substance in a land that hates its foreigners
while laying claim to them like property. Half
a man.

Even here—lost in space—with mythic constellations turned
      on their ears,
the sky a black balloon swooning endlessly into itself,
planets named for the half-men, half-beasts of ancient Greece—
even here, Doctor Smith's a foreign body
whose secret dreams of hydroponic garden boys
are coolly scrutinized by stars.

Sometimes he imagines his heart is Saturn, everything
he desires on a silver platter of dust particles and ice
swirling endlessly around a land mass
of enormous consequence.

BY-THE-WIND-SAILOR

Orion stomps across the windowpane—
"Watch your ass, baby, or I'll take my belt off to you!"

"Those damned gods and their tantrums!"
Stars pause in passing like clean white sailor's

caps upon the starched black cotton laps
of invisible sailors who—still

invisible—drunkenly rise and drunkenly
amble back across the sky. Their moves are smooth

but never amiable on nights so cold
the bark of earth pulls tight around its tree.

The World: impoverished, cranky, at the mercy
of flowers and sailors. Sad World, above whom

the gods, like indivisible numerals, storm
angrily to and fro, frustrated with we

who see only stars. Between the burning,
hard-to-handle pinpricks of constellated light

beleaguered night with its thankless involvements
wears itself out behind the scenes like Vitrolite,

that sublime architectural glass whose popularity
was so inexplicably brief: 1926 to '39—a short life span

for a celestial glass upon which opalescent hues
—tomato-silver, lunar green—cast a chilling, gaseous

sheen as if on smoothed tinfoil. Brimming with resentment,
unrecognized night goes about its daily affairs

knowing it ought to pull back, but can't. Lack
of discipline? Force of habit? A power greater than oneself?

Night cries into its shimmering, headless bier,
"I'm bloody tired of holding the whole damn thing together!"

Behind infinity's black scrim, By-the-Wind-Sailors gather,
condensing and running together as thoughtlessly as milk,

before (like gods) revising their plans, and drifting off again
in search of slightly less portentous spheres.

SKY PARTY

They floated like bubbles in the air,
the tiny ones ensnared, released by sponges
immersed and uplifted by dishwashing suds—
nothing like the fat glass peaches kids exhale
through store-bought plastic hoops.

Flying poodles—opalescent, minuscule—
with fancy topiary poodle 'dos:
baubled legs, tails, heads, clean-shaven
snouts noiselessly snorkeling the atmosphere,
and spines curled back like unfurling fiddleheads of fern

so that after watching them awhile
they distilled into seahorses—
a herd of poodle seahorses—
drifting arrogantly by.

GARGOYLE

Laryngitis, lozenges, soda jerks.
Things sound alike. And are.

We, for instance, began as fountains,
named for our absentminded *gargle*.
Or *cloud*—from *gloutos*, Greek for buttock—
vanilla folds of buffered foam.

Instead of a soda jerk at the Fountain of Decay
I long to be high flung, a skyscraper's burning scrape.
Head in clouds, wings rolled tight as tabloids
from a stone-cold sober world: editions early, final, late.

Inside my mouth no tongue. Who needs a tongue,
the water's dulling swoon? I dream of bone-dry eyes
that smudge and smooth horizon with a sharp,
        unblinking glare,
taking in the airborne bridges between bird of prey and prayer.

I dream of hunchback shoulder blades of predatory stone—
where peregrines build, then abandon to me their
        thorny crowns.
Some office worker joker sticks a cigarette in my mouth.
Clouds tamp it out.

At my feet a skyline kingdom of blue-black stacks of ash
pliable as ashen sheaths, and acid rain emulsions
rinsing from the city's skin. This fountain's
ultimate revenge: *to drink the city in.*

RE-FORESTATION

*A dog
and a friendly
voice that calls,
"He's friendly."*
—FROM JAMES SCHUYLER'S "THE WALK"

Detonating
dandelion orbs
impress you,
their pollen
zithering away
on the wind's
downstream.
Vizslas are
the dog
of the hour,
supplanting
rotties and
even goldens.
I'll never forget
the puppy
weimaraner
that first summer
with Otto—
it galloped dopily

from the woods,
a whorl of ears,
lichen gray:
like fog induced
to mammal form.

They've fenced
those woods off
now to restore
Brooklyn's "last
intact
wilderness."
We stand
at its margins
staring past
the rude
impromptu
gate at the
red-winged
blackbirds nesting
in the pond's
tall reeds.
"How soft
those bods
must be," you say,
"to emit such
delicate eggs."

I think you're
envious.

In a naked tree
a young hawk
with speckled breast
calls to mama,
dive-bombed
by blue jays.
Blowing
the heads off
soft white
dandelion lobes
(color of spent
lightbulbs),
discussing lunch
and Brian's
failing health,
we try to envision
a time when
all of this—
all—was
solid woods,
while Otto
sinks between us
like mortar,
fur the color of

papaya meat
in sunlight,
starkly enunciated
against the pearl-
black seeds of
toenails, muzzle,
paw pads, brow.
"This is love
and sorrow
mixed:
a world
of grand
misgivings."
The potent
uselessness
of words:
re-forestation,
Brian at home
with a mouth
full of sores,
our failing love,
the anxious intent
of pollen
and the wind
that gambles it.

NESTS IN WINTER TREES

I love how trees' limbs express wind,
emulating the invisible vectors
of the atmosphere's momentum—
manifesting any given moment's
unrepeatable gift, its lessons
in balance and leaning.

Every twenty trees or so
one notes a dark spot,
a brittle coagulation, as if
a brain were forming in the niche
of transversing branches—a mind
materializing to dream up
things entirely new
for a tree to do

—or the embodiment
of remembering something
ancient or forbidden: a falling
apple, gravity, the rope-burn pull
of the wrongly accused.

The minds of old branches
fill with the remains of older trees,
with lichen, hair, and fishing line,

all twined by an industry of birds
in tangled ovals of complex memory

like horses merging in a tight corral's stampede.

THE WILLIAMSBURGH SAVINGS BANK

Autumn returns the clock tower to my window.
All summer long, I imagined four clocks, three times as high
as my ceiling, timepieces large as time, receding behind
    serrated leaves.

A snowy owl lived there last winter, an attaché of night.
I first saw him while speeding up Flatbush Avenue—
orbiting the golden dome, brilliant white in floodlights,

a circumambulating monk, a soaring foreground
barely affixed to the dark sky behind him.
One night I watched him from my window, diving for mice.

And once, walking by, barely heard the velvet mumble
    of his flight
as he spiraled down to seize his prey, first swaddling
it in an alabaster flash of wings, then stillness spread

across the bloodless scream, ascending at last with talons
tight and full, like the pulleyed weight of a pendulum clock,
as if the tower were calling him back.

BREAKING THE ELEPHANT

You ask him how the elephants,
which you have ridden in the jungle today,
are trained.

He tells you how they capture them.
How traps are set for the elephants
but the elephants, being clever,
avoid the traps. So the men
set off firecrackers in the jungle
and this "terrifies the elephants
and makes them forget the traps."
How a captured elephant is kept
in a deep ditch for days, unfed
for days, then finally fed
and given water by the men,
"so she will learn to trust people."
The elephant stays alone
in the ditch for weeks,
fed and watered by the people
she has come to depend upon.

At last she is led from
the ditch to observe
a trained elephant at work.
At first the new elephant

will not know what to do—
"She will not understand
because she is still too innocent."
Then the trainer begins
to break the elephant.
He hits the elephant—"beats
the elephant"—on the head,
on the convex head of an Indian
elephant, so unlike the head
of an African elephant, whose
head is concave, whose ears
are shaped like the continent
of Africa. He does it
with a heavy stick
or a hook of iron.

The trainer continues
to break the elephant.
He cuts or pierces her ears—
the most sensitive part
of an elephant's body—ears
she flaps to cool herself,
ears which her trainer will grasp
to hoist himself up
along her trunk,
ears pink and gray,
thinner than a human earlobe.

The trainer hurts the elephant, you are told,
"so the elephant will remember
what a person can do."
He injures her, lets her heal,
then cuts her again.
He shows you the scars
on the elephant's head,
the slashes in her ear—
"so the elephant learns," he says.

And you ask about that sound
the ones behind the hut
are making, a tremulous,
urgent roar, as if something important
were being discussed, then broadcast.
"What does it mean?" you ask.
And he tells you,

"That is the sound they make when they are happy."

DEPICTING THE THRUSH SONG

How precise do you want it?

The thrush down the block's
long row of backyard gardens
sounded like the sad slurring
of a song half sung,
moistened fingers rounding
a wineglass rim,
or an old porch door, broken-
screened, squeaky hinged,
opening and closing on a field of black pansies.

A mournful whistle we only
hear in morning's first moments
or the long day's last—at dusk
a liquid gate eased shut,
careening waterfall
of rising syllables:

in-com-plete
in-com-plete
in-com-plete

IV

THE LIGHT
MOVING
BEHIND IT

QUIETUS

The word is quietus,
leaning like a tree.
A tilted tombstone
uplifting earth,
a slow shovel's delve.

Late afternoon
birds land on
the word,
bend its q's and u's,
quake its t's—
trembling branches
on which ale-colored
shadows tremble.

The earth swallows
the sun like a lozenge,
again. On another side
of the word, sun
swallows earth.

Quietus, a typeface,
loops its script on stone,
a sieve to pass through
like the letter q,

a rose lasso,
or a butler with a rose lapel,
helping us out of the formalwear of flesh.

QUINCE

stars annotate stars
as the imagined quince tree—
now gone—annotates

memories padlocked
to one another, the
borough of Brooklyn

locked to Queens, link to
link to a bird song back to:
"you're getting warmer"

as in "closer," as in
an Easter egg hunt
conducted at dusk.

what you feel, learn to
unfeel. unravel that big
blunt heart, its heart string.

high above, the big
and little bears awash in
stars' distant, oily hues

peppermint pastels

just out of reach (see them! smell
them!) are not unlike

flowering branches
of quince (terse word, quince,
like quinine stabbed through

by dark scarlet darts)
whose meteors resemble
petals peeling off

in liquid streaks of
bleachy pink: spring unravels
in increments like

the turning wheel of
constellations, seasons, nights,
cities, and lives so

far gone, empty, and
condensed they erupt in quince
and aching.

[After Joseph Cornell]

THE BAT STUDY

The biology professor struggles
to disentangle the little bat
from the mist net, rescuing
it from a capture he contrived.

It's the third bat tonight,
but the first female,
her soft brown back spanned
by two vanilla-colored bands
stretching like suspenders
from her shoulders to her feet.

She's pregnant, the professor says,
and sure enough, there's a little belly there.

He extends her wings,
membrane accordions in
an inky Japanese cartoon.
The flashlight beam projects
as if through black rice paper.
The bones in those wings twitch—
she's trying to unflex them,
to fold them around her three-inch frame
of fur and fear, but he holds fast.
Her eyes squeeze shut, open wide, and flash.

She twists her head to bite his hand—
how can she know what this is about,
this studious terror that means no harm?
Her teeth sink into the flashlit air.
Her face, no larger than his thumb,
furrows with frustration.

The other students want to touch, study her,
they aim their cameras
and flash until she squints,
then turns her face away, disgraced.

The professor hands her around.
The second student says,
I think I've torn the wing.

WHAT I TAKE INTO THE DARK

This yellow handrail leads
to the mouth of the tunnel
where the barn owl, chased
by a mob of mid-day commuters,
smooth-sailed on wings of silent, skimming
cream. What is this life that disappears
into simple darkness, followed by hurling
stones, and reappears in the vectors
of sleep, the vistas of dilated pupils,
the planes, differentials, and right angles
of everything we think we know,
segmented into quadrants: one side the near future,
another, the immediate vicinity of everything we love?

I call your dead name and something alights in me,
wings aloof to the heart's straining harpsichord—
the owl passes through pale strings as if
through a stand of birch
and stirs no sound.

What I take into the dark is
what I will remember
about you. It is a quiet thing,
all I can carry with one fist
on the handrail, sliding along

its smooth cylinder into
the land of things retained
and given flight. We are coming
to know this land well. We are often
chased into it by mobs
or memories of mobs.

If we could photograph this land
perhaps we could convey it to the others.
What good would that do?
Even in photos the dark
is a chemical compound, soluble
as a night bird in night branches
on a moonless, heaving hill.

PROPERTIES

Glass is a liquid,
spilling over time.
Slower than molasses slow.

Let's walk that hill
behind the house
all the way back
to the abandoned barn.
It's old.
The blues and grays
and foamy whites
painted long ago
are barely chips now,
tiny islands
on a splintered sea,
crumbs that ants
might tug
with swollen mandibles,
or the eggs of ants.

Behind these walls,
cows ate and dreamt,
were milked by hand for years,
and later, by kettle machines
that hung by straps

across their backs.
They dropped silvery calves
on this cemented sawdust floor,
bending to lick their nostrils clear,
to taste their taste.
On cold mornings, the calves' bodies
sent up steam, signaling.

It's barely morning now.
They'd be waking,
here and in the house.
Lights, first upstairs,
then down,
their bedroom and their kitchen.

But here's what I wanted you to see:
this slow dripping pane
narrow at the top
and at the bottom, thick,
as if an animal were hibernating,
invisible, in the glass.
A snake. A slug.
A cloud, stretched out.

PULLING OUT OF METUCHIN ON THE 4:43

The oysterous clouds, which have been at it
all day, finally part company, emitting
a clear metallic ray angled
like an escalator from there to here.

In this, the hour when something always shines,
what is it we are searching for?
Oyster-lipped suitcases dangle
from the heavy hands
of exhausted travelers who long
to ride that floating escalator's
distant, precision silver,
identical to the fish-quick shine
of yesterday's Chrysler Building
emerging from fog. Glancing
east on Forty-second Street,
the enormous "Tudor City" sign towered
like directions to a place
only an escalator of light could reach,
a shimmering dirigible, a healed-up scar.

You will need your oyster suitcase
to travel there, a longitude
to follow to the end of the day,
that seemingly endless commute

in one unsettling direction,
then all the way back again
as this day sutures itself to yet another.

LOVE AFTER DEATH

Light shone through the empty clamshells on the sand
illuminating them like rawhide lamps.
From there we could see the city.

We smelled her on the air
like an Aladdin cologne
mounting carpets of pollen, scaling ocean spray walls.

My dog watched the air,
his gaze shifting from side to side,
following the movements of an invisible companion.

We listen at the passage
of the city of our pillows
for insistent heartbeats thumping
between zipper and foam rubber.

The city a city of semipermeable structures.
The city a city of old dogs curled on blankets.
Of clamshells, lanterns, unzipped Aladdins.
Of bonemeal, pollen, invisible companions.

For L., in memory of Jesse

VASE EPIPHANIES

After you left   I kissed the tulips you gave me   till the petals
fell   from their stems   then kissed   their fallen half-shells
pink and steamy white   caressed them   curled on the floor
my cheeks against their angel knees   I gathered them together
took them to bed   but couldn't sleep   they made me
nocturnal   eyes wide as tulips cooked   in darkness my
petals   peeling away   from their stems   disengaging from
a very close thing   I too   in free-fall   I too   nuzzled while
vaguely dying   absorbed   in a tea cup's pleasant frailty   I too
a petal canoe   touched   lifted   laid   in the current   godlike
in new tremendousness   an oracle   worshiped with kisses
in the final moments   of the coming apart   of all the parts
fragrance great   and   finite   longing beyond   the reach   of
longing   love beyond   the grasp   of love

DREAM

I dreamed I had a fireplace
and that you slept beside me there.
I watched us as if from another body,
and longed to be me, warm in the blaze of resting
against you.

I dreamed of what wakefulness excluded,
of dust motes in air, those tiny hope motels
made incandescent by negligee light.

I dreamed the light was alive.

I dreamed you drank oat tea in the 4 a.m. dark,
the white cup traveling from lips
to lap like a satellite.
I read you poetry and kissed you above
a copper book's soft cover,
over and over.

I dreamed of the raven's first call
from its branch outside my window,
so close, and of those black feathers ruffling
under insinuations of wind.

I dreamed of the first light's hesitant grain
moistly suckling the window pane behind the white shade.

I dreamed we talked of honey and lions,
of home-grown watercress,
ex-lovers and their ex's.

I dreamed you said, "You make it hard
not to love you."

After that I couldn't sleep.

For A.

THERE

In the dark it was exciting,
the knowing and not knowing:

that an eclipse was coming
but not quite exactly

what an eclipse was.
Amidst the friction of the words

"lunar eclipse" was the longing
to hear it explained again and

again, a telling and re-telling,
a form of caressing:

solar, partial, total, full.
It was the thrill of show and tell,

of digging out the old baseball,
the Eveready flashlight, and one

cool pink grapefruit from the crisper.
As you switched off the kitchen light,

I raised the baseball at arm's
length above me, the grapefruit before

my face, like a face I might some-
day kiss, and you stood nearby

in the kitchen's blank stillness—
its stacks of plates and bowls, its bent silver tines—

and switched the flashlight on
so its beam angled like a downward

skid of spider web, then roved the dark wall
till you found Earth, and shone it there,

and cast a conquering shadow on its moon.
It's the vibrant chafing click

of that Eveready flashlight switching
on, there, in the dark with you,

while holding a baseball and a fruit,
that I remember best

a memory as possessive of itself
as a planet of its moon, eclipsing everything else:

even its own brightest moments,
which, lo, the conquering shadows hold aloft.

THE NEARNESS OF YOU

I. The Waiting Room
Jellybeans fill a festive jar, their pale oceanic hues
carbonate the fluid denial that halfway through the wait
implodes, bubble on a pin: *I know.*

I know, but return my gaze to *Connoisseur*,
its gloss turned suddenly sinister—
a hard-boiled Wim Wenders,
dancing bears, tornadoes on amateur video,
the effect of "swear words" on the young.
Bryan Miller drones food reviews on WQXR,
Canby pans Stallone, then Magic Johnson on "avoiding" AIDS.

The emaciated receptionist stage-whispers advice to an
        emaciated Latino man.
The blonde sitting beside me furiously studies *Mad*,
his arm a field of clotted violets.

Time stands on its head 'til you appear in the doorway,
a white bag in hand, more tests to pass or fail.
You smile at me, but your face is pale.
Fragmented murmurs to the receptionist:
T-cell, Tuesday, checkbook, blood test.
He's seen it all a thousand times, but still
he's flustered: "Refrigerate the sample in the radiator,"

he repeats three times to get the words to come out right.
They won't.
It's a long, dumb moment that only ends
when you put an end to it: "It's OK,"
you say, "I think I've got it."

II. The Street

Cold. Dark. Wet. A winter noir cliché. You're shivering.
The sound of chattering teeth so intimate, amplified by
how little attention I've paid all this time
to the body's small sounds. The sound
of your cigarette is strike, ignite, inhale.
"It's not the best of news," you say, voice also pale.

We sleepwalk east from West Tenth Street,
past tranquil brownstones whose pristine
windows on married life
I long to fracture with stones tonight—
those living rooms insult us
with their virtuous amber light
suspended like epithets by the moisture in the air.
I hope they're nice and fucking warm in there,
I think, as my hand finds yours.
"It's OK," you say, but you don't pull away.
"I know it is. I would've done this anyway."
Only the first part, we both know, a lie.

III. The Nearness of You

Your place, as always, smells like
sandalwood, talc, and oatmeal soap.
In the kitchen, cranberry cocktails shimmer
in tall glasses like votive candles before us.
Our words rise like bubbles in the cool fluorescent air:
yours pop, mine pop, they amount to nothing.
Like a mantra you're repeating, "It'll all be OK."

When Annie phones, I'm relieved for a moment alone
in your living room to gaze, slow-brained,
at the blue TV special
on Sarah Vaughan's early days.
"I've been to the doctor," I overhear you say.
Silvery footage of spotlight, curtain, stage.
"Not good." Your voice sounds far away.
Sarah steps up to the mike and the band begins to play
the now-familiar phrase: "I tested positive today."

From your window Manhattan's inflamed with the blues.
The song Sarah's singing is *The Nearness of You*.

For S.

BOTANICAL GARDENS AT NIGHT

After Pablo Neruda's "Ode with a Lament"

I.

Dogs' teeth and lightbulbs
make a sacred crown around all the letters
I carry but never send.
Here in the dark, awaiting delivery
I lick myself like a foreign stamp,
obtuse drawing of an obscure bloom.

II.

And if I carry my letters to the dead,
the undead, the ones who want me dead, all of us dead,
who always seem to live,
and the ones who gave us life, who loved us,
then turned us away?
If I deliver my X-rayed flowers, my anatomical charts,
maps of earth and skin and sky on unshackled walls?
But the dead are among us, the living in hiding.
And the names of the flora and fauna have changed,
borders shifted, cities dissolved,
and the foreign bodies' names have changed.
And heavenly bodies have lost their names.
Anatomy and physics and physical love have changed.

III.

The life preserver, round as candy
hangs from a white hook on the outer wall
of an unlit boat house, a peppermint
darkening in the rain, a luminous sphere of moss
cut with a pen knife. Something you said
that I can't remember. Something rained away.

IV.

I long for him the way ghosts
long for tulips or barnacles,
for their box of white moths,
for the sweaty canal of the heart
where dreams dock their houseboats.
Thoughts of his death press
like warm putty
lifting the newsprint from my pages,
carting off my brave cartoons.

Oh, how I long to see him, how I miss him in advance.

V.

The crossing of the river.
The falling out of bed.
The taste of marble.
Curling tusk of a mastodon.
Snow on your black shoe.

"She wants to be dead," you said,
"and I want to be a volcano."

VI.

Unlit houses on a midnight hill.
White lanterns beneath the drain pipe.
The salt water underpass.
"I never had any children," he told me,
"Survival was my child."

VII.

Wisteria the color of plums held underwater,
uncertainly blue, as if blue were a lantern
wielding a type of light that could be carried
like a baby or an ice cube tray
from room to room.
Or a blue-frosted cake without a ticket.
Or the clean blue smell of saccharine.
"I no longer love you," was what you said.

VIII.

Pheasants strut among the brambles.
A children's book with the pages torn out
floats face up in the lily pad pond.
A note in the grass
written in a child's black chalk hand
reads: "white spider."

I am locked in you again tonight,
a lesbian botanist in the statuary
of motorcycles, mushroom caps, and pitbulls.
An axis and a sundial in a long, longing field
of lambs, paperweights, and lamp shades.
A pillar of salt the deer come to lick
for electrolytes and sonnets.

IX.

She is a doorway made of churning wheat
which my mouth can neither open nor close.
I feed on the things that take my breath away:
petrified crutches and letters to Jesus,
doves and white chairs oddly placed in the meadow,
handcuffs and ice floes and broken chess pieces.

And the lichens, algae, primates of your heart.

X.

Dim weeds pinch the startled
columns of ginkgo and black pine
that tower like twisted book shelves
of mysteries, Bibles, and porn.
Red worms twitch in the black water like party favors
when flashlights beam through them.
The dark puts its soft finger on the light

until the light is as weak
as an ash or a tricycle in the rain.

There is a hotel lobby in my heart.
Full of sleepwalkers and jars of ivy.
A lobby of bellhops and pens with no language.
A lobby of mint with a shiny black filling.
Inside the lobby a hothouse with baking glass.
Oh little dove of the burning bakery,
oh towering owl of soda water and dust,
open your wings to me,
reunite me with the sky—
for the clouds move so quickly,
though they carry whole cities
though they carry this garden
underneath their damp sighs.

NOTES

PAGE 18
Loop-the-Loop in Prospect Park (1905)

This poem was inspired by a photograph in George Chauncey's *Gay New York: Gender, Urban Culture, and the Making of the Gay Male World, 1890-1940*, in which Chauncey writes: "[A] female impersonator from a poor neighborhood in Brooklyn where he was known as Loop-the-loop, a suggestive play on the name of a popular ride at Coney Island, reported to a doctor in 1906 that he regularly plied his trade 'chiefly for the money there is in it.' Loop-the-loop often worked in his neighborhood as well as in Prospect Park, where, he reported, he and the other prostitutes paid off the patrolmen so that they could wear dresses" (pp. 68-69). Additional information about Prospect Park in Loop-the-loop's time came from the following sources: *Brooklyn...And How It Got That Way*, David McCullough; *Prospect Park: From Grand Army Plaza to Garden Terrace via Swan Boat Lake: A Walking Tour,* Notes by Henry Hope Reed, Jr. (June 6, 1965); and *The Peet Book on Trees* (1902).

PAGE 45
For Brandon Teena

Brandon Teena was a biological female who passed as a young man in Lincoln and in Falls City, Nebraska. In 1993, she was raped and murdered by two men after her transgenderism was forcibly exposed. She was twenty-one years old.

ABOUT THE AUTHOR

Gerry Gomez Pearlberg is a poet and editor whose writings have been widely anthologized in such places as *Women on Women 3*, *Hers 2*, *Queer View Mirror 2*, and *Sister and Brother*. A winner of the 1993 Judith's Room Emerging Women Poets Award, she has edited three poetry anthologies: *The Key to Everything: Classic Lesbian Love Poems* (a Lambda Book Award Nominee, *The Zenith of Desire: Contemporary Lesbian Poems About Sex*, and most recently, *Queer Dog: Homo/ Pup/Poetry* (Cleis, 1997). She lives in Brooklyn, New York.

Queer Dog
HOMO/PUP/POETRY

Edited by Gerry Gomez Pearlberg

"Why do gay men and lesbians have so much to say
on the subject of dogs?
Perhaps because we're masters at re-configuring
what it means to create family,
what it means to be animal and living in skin,
what it means to exist in a state of exuberant,
unapologetic disobedience."

— GERRY GOMEZ PEARLBERG

Jack Anderson / W.H. Auden / Robin Becker / Mark Bibbins / Joe Brainard / James Broughton / Ana Marie Castañon / Justin Chin / Jeffery Conway / Bernard Cooper / Dennis Cooper / Chrystos / Gavin Geoffrey Dillard / Tim Dlugos / Mark Doty / Angie Estes / Edward Field / Jan Freeman / Eliza Galaher / Timothy Gerken / Melinda Goodman / Thom Gunn / Richard Harteis / Eloise Klein Healy / Melanie Hope / Michael Klein / Wayne Koestenbaum / Michael Lassell / David Levinson / Timothy Liu / Jules Mann / Judith McDaniel / Honor Moore / Carl Morse / Eileen Myles / Adrian Oktenberg / Gerry Gomez Pearlberg / John Del Peschio / Aleida Rodríguez / May Sarton / Lawrence Schimel / James Schuyler / Robyn Selman / Linda Smukler / Gertrude Stein / May Swenson / David Trinidad / Kitty Tsui / Jennifer Willoughby / Fran Winant / Terry Wolverton / Gerard Wozek / Eva Yaa Asantewaa

Read it to your favorite pup tonight!

BOOKS FROM CLEIS PRESS

DEBUT LITERATURE

Marianne Faithfull's Cigarette
by Gerry Gomez Pearlberg.
ISBN: 1-57344-034-5   12.95 paper.

Memory Mambo
by Achy Obejas.
LAMBDA LITERARY AWARD WINNER.
ISBN: 1-57344-017-5   12.95 paper.

*We Came All The Way from Cuba
So You Could Dress Like This?:
Stories* by Achy Obejas.
LAMBDA LITERARY AWARD WINNER.
ISBN: 0-939416-93-X   10.95 paper.

Seeing Dell by Carol Guess.
ISBN: 1-57344-023-X   12.95 paper.

LESBIAN AND GAY STUDIES

*The Case of the Good-For-
Nothing Girlfriend*
by Mabel Maney.
LAMBDA LITERARY AWARD NOMINEE.
ISBN: 0-939416-91-3   10.95 paper.

The Case of the Not-So-Nice Nurse
by Mabel Maney.
LAMBDA LITERARY AWARD NOMINEE.
ISBN: 0-939416-76-X   9.95 paper.

Nancy Clue and the Hardly
Boys in *A Ghost in the Closet*
by Mabel Maney.
LAMBDA LITERARY AWARD NOMINEE.
ISBN: 1-57344-012-4   10.95 paper.

*Different Daughters:
A Book by Mothers of Lesbians,*
second edition,
edited by Louise Rafkin.
ISBN: 1-57344-050-7   12.95 paper.

*Different Mothers:
Sons & Daughters of Lesbians
Talk about Their Lives,*
edited by Louise Rafkin.
LAMBDA LITERARY AWARD WINNER.
ISBN: 0-939416-41-7   9.95 paper.

A Lesbian Love Advisor
by Celeste West.
ISBN: 0-939416-26-3   9.95 paper.

On the Rails: A Memoir,
second edition, by Linda
Niemann. Introduction by
Leslie Marmon Silko.
ISBN: 1-57344-064-7.   14.95 paper.

Queer Dog: Homo Pup Poetry,
edited by Gerry Gomez
Pearlberg.
ISBN: 1-57344-071-X.   12.95. paper.

WORLD LITERATURE

A Forbidden Passion
by Cristina Peri Rossi.
ISBN: 0-939416-68-9   9.95 paper.

*Half a Revolution: Contemporary
Fiction by Russian Women,*
edited by Masha Gessen.
ISBN 1-57344-006-X $12.95 paper.

*The Little School:
Tales of Disappearance and
Survival in Argentina*
by Alicia Partnoy.
ISBN: 0-939416-07-7   9.95 paper.

*Peggy Deery: An Irish
Family at War*
by Nell McCafferty.
ISBN: 0-939416-39-5   9.95 paper.

THRILLERS & DYSTOPIAS

Another Love
by Erzsébet Galgóczi.
ISBN: 0-939416-51-4   8.95 paper.

*Dirty Weekend: A Novel of
Revenge*
by Helen Zahavi.
ISBN: 0-939416-85-9   10.95 paper.

Only Lawyers Dancing
by Jan McKemmish.
ISBN: 0-939416-69-7   9.95 paper.

The Wall by Marlen Haushofer.
ISBN: 0-939416-54-9   9.95 paper.

VAMPIRES & HORROR

*Brothers of the Night: Gay
Vampire Stories*
edited by Michael Rowe and
Thomas S. Roche.
ISBN: 1-57344-025-6   14.95 paper.

*Dark Angels: Lesbian Vampire
Stories,*
edited by Pam Keesey.
LAMBDA LITERARY AWARD NOMINEE.
ISBN 1-7344-014-0   10.95 paper.

*Daughters of Darkness: Lesbian
Vampire Stories,*
edited by Pam Keesey.
ISBN: 0-939416-78-6   9.95 paper.

*Vamps: An Illustrtated History of
the Femme Fatale*
by Pam Keesey.
ISBN: 1-57344-026-4   21.95.

*Sons of Darkness: Tales of Men,
Blood and Immortality,*
edited by Michael Rowe and
Thomas S. Roche.
LAMBDA LITERARY AWARD NOMINEE.
ISBN: 1-57344-059-0   12.95 paper.

*Women Who Run with the
Werewolves: Tales of Blood, Lust
and Metamorphosis,*
edited by Pam Keesey.
LAMBDA LITERARY AWARD NOMINEE.
ISBN: 1-57344-057-4   12.95 paper.

GENDER TRANSGRESSION

Body Alchemy: Transsexual Portraits by Loren Cameron.
LAMBDA LITERARY AWARD WINNER.
ISBN: 1-57344-062-0   24.95 paper.

Dagger: On Butch Women, edited by Roxxie, Lily Burana, Linnea Due.
ISBN: 0-939416-82-4   14.95 paper.

I Am My Own Woman: The Outlaw Life of Charlotte von Mahlsdorf,
translated by Jean Hollander.
ISBN: 1-57344-010-8   12.95 paper.

Sex Changes: The Politics of Transgenderism by Pat Califia
ISBN: 1-57344-072-8   16.95 paper.

SEXUAL POLITICS

Forbidden Passages: Writings Banned in Canada,
introductions by Pat Califia and Janine Fuller.
LAMBDA LITERARY AWARD WINNER.
ISBN: 1-57344-019-1   14.95 paper.

PoMoSexuals: Challenging Assumptions about Gender and Sexuality
edited by Carol Queen and Lawrence Schimel.
Preface by Kate Bornstein.
ISBN: 1-57344-074-4   14.95 paper.

Public Sex: The Culture of Radical Sex by Pat Califia.
ISBN: 0-939416-89-1   12.95 paper.

Real Live Nude Girl: Chronicles of Sex-Positive Culture
by Carol Queen.
ISBN: 1-57344-073-6.   14.95 paper.

Sex Work: Writings by Women in the Sex Industry,
edited by Frédérique Delacoste and Priscilla Alexander.
ISBN: 0-939416-11-5   16.95 paper.

Susie Bright's Sexual Reality: A Virtual Sex World Reader
by Susie Bright.
ISBN: 0-939416-59-X   9.95 paper.

Susie Bright's Sexwise
by Susie Bright.
ISBN: 1-57344-002-7   10.95 paper.

Susie Sexpert's Lesbian Sex World
by Susie Bright.
ISBN: 0-939416-35-2   9.95 paper.

EROTIC LITERATURE

Best Gay Erotica 1998,
selected by Christopher Bram, edited by Richard Labonté.
ISBN: 1-57344-031-0   14.95 paper.

Best Gay Erotica 1997,
selected by Douglas Sadownick, edited by Richard Labonté.
ISBN: 1-57344-067-1   14.95 paper.

Best Gay Erotica 1996,
selected by Scott Heim,
edited by Michael Ford.
ISBN: 1-57344-052-3   12.95 paper.

Best Lesbian Erotica 1998,
selected by Jenifer Levin,
edited by Tristan Taormino.
ISBN: 1-57344-032-9   14.95 paper.

Best Lesbian Erotica 1997,
selected by Jewelle Gomez,
edited by Tristan Taormino.
ISBN: 1-57344-065-5   14.95 paper.

Serious Pleasure: Lesbian Erotic Stories and Poetry,
edited by the Sheba Collective.
ISBN: 0-939416-45-X   9.95 paper.

Switch Hitters: Lesbians Write Gay Male Erotica and Gay Men Write Lesbian Erotica,
edited by Carol Queen and Lawrence Schimel.
ISBN: 1-57344-021-3   12.95 paper.

WRITER'S REFERENCE

Putting Out: The Essential Publishing Resource Guide For Gay and Lesbian Writers, fourth edition, by Edisol W. Dotson.
ISBN: 1-57344-033-7   14.95 paper.

POLITICS OF HEALTH

The Absence of the Dead Is Their Way of Appearing
by Mary Winfrey Trautmann.
ISBN: 0-939416-04-2   8.95 paper.

Don't: A Woman's Word
by Elly Danica.
ISBN: 0-939416-22-0   8.95 paper

Voices in the Night: Women Speaking About Incest,
edited by Toni A.H. McNaron and Yarrow Morgan.
ISBN: 0-939416-02-6   9.95 paper.

With the Power of Each Breath: A Disabled Women's Anthology,
edited by Susan Browne, Debra Connors and Nanci Stern.
ISBN: 0-939416-06-9   10.95 paper.

TRAVEL & COOKING

Betty and Pansy's Severe Queer Review of New York
by Betty Pearl and Pansy.
ISBN: 1-57344-070-1   10.95 paper.

Betty and Pansy's Severe Queer Review of San Francisco
by Betty Pearl and Pansy.
ISBN: 1-57344-056-6   10.95 paper.

Food for Life & Other Dish,
edited by Lawrence Schimel.
ISBN: 1-57344-061-2   14.95 paper.